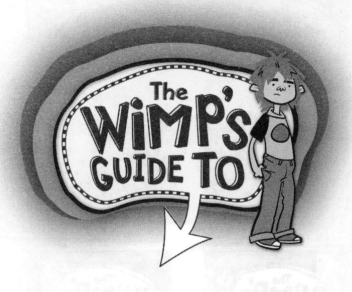

978 1 4451 1460 6 pb   978 1 4451 1464 4 eBook

978 1 4451 1461 3 pb   978 1 4451 1465 1 eBook

978 1 4451 1458 3 pb   9781445114620 eBook

978 1 4451 1459 0 pb   978 1 4451 1463 7 eBook

illustrated by
Dave Smith

Extreme SPORTS

by
Tracey Turner

EDGE
FRANKLIN WATTS

LONDON·SYDNEY

First published in 2013
by Franklin Watts

Text © Tracey Turner 2013
Illustrations by Dave Smith
© Franklin Watts 2013
Cover design by Cathryn Gilbert
Layout by Jonathan Hair

Franklin Watts
338 Euston Road
London NW1 3BH

Franklin Watts Australia
Level 17/207 Kent Street
Sydney, NSW 2000

A CIP catalogue record for this book
is available from the British Library.

(Library ebook) ISBN: 978 1 4451 2574 9
(pb) ISBN: 978 1 4451 1460 6
(ebook) ISBN: 978 1 4451 1464 4

1 3 5 7 9 10 8 6 4 2

Printed in Great Britain

*WARNING:
Extreme sports should
only be practised under
expert supervision.

*The Publisher and Author accept no liability
for loss or injury sustained as a result of
reading this book. So you've been warned!

Franklin Watts is
a division of Hachette
Children's Books, an
Hachette UK company.

www.hachette.co.uk

CONTENTS

INTRODUCTION

There's nothing wrong with being a wimp. It makes perfect sense to be scared when, for example, you're plummeting down an almost vertical ski slope, or dangling over a gaping abyss suspended by a piece of elastic.

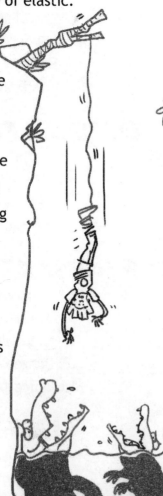

There's a wimp inside all of us, and he or she is there for a very good reason — to stop us from doing dangerous stuff. Despite the obvious hazards of jumping off very tall things or sliding down slippery stuff, some people are determined to seek adrenalin-fuelled adventure in the form of extreme sports. And there's a surprisingly wide variety of perilous stuff to do. . .

LEAPING FROM AEROPLANES

CYCLING DOWN VIOLENT VOLCANOES

KAYAKING DOWN ROARING RAPIDS

...and many more.

Prepare yourself, because we're about to take a white-knuckle ride through the world of extreme sports, dicing with danger and staring death straight in the eye. Though some of us might have to look through our fingers...

And just in case, maybe you should put on...

...a safety helmet...

...a life-jacket...

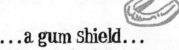

...a gum shield...

...knee pads...

...and a safety harness.

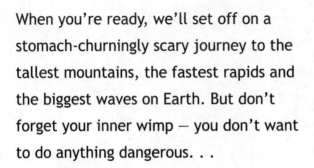

When you're ready, we'll set off on a stomach-churningly scary journey to the tallest mountains, the fastest rapids and the biggest waves on Earth. But don't forget your inner wimp — you don't want to do anything dangerous. . .

EXTREME SPORTS: ON LAND

Dry land sounds like a pretty safe place to be — until you start hurtling down really steep bits of it at more than 250 kph, or performing impossible-looking tricks on bikes.

Extreme Bikes

Maybe you ride your bike to school. Perhaps, when you're feeling brave, you might cycle into the countryside, where you fearlessly ride along designated cycle paths. You have probably never considered careering down steep slopes littered with jagged rocks and slippery mud banks, negotiating boulders and even wild animals. . .

BELIEVE IT OR NOT. . .

Mountain biker Robert Mennen was competing in the Cape Epic cross-country event in South Africa in 2013, when he encountered an unusual hazard: he was knocked off his bike by an antelope. The 60 kph crash broke the handlebars of Robert's bike and damaged his left collarbone, but fortunately both he and the antelope recovered.

He didn't see that coming!

Mountain Biking

This doesn't mean cycling down mountains — that would be really dangerous...

Oh, hang on a minute — actually it does mean cycling down mountains!

If you're hard enough, downhill cycling is one of the mountain-bike events hard-as-nails riders can compete in, and they cycle down actual mountains, as fast as they can.

Other mountain-bike events include:

Cross country (which is the most popular, and possibly the most gruelling)

Dirt jumping (jumping over mounds of earth — but on your bike, which is a lot trickier)

Trials (mountain-bike obstacle courses)

DOWNHILL CYCLING VITAL STATISTICS

◦ Races are against the clock and courses usually take five minutes or less to complete — but it's an interesting five minutes.

◦ Some ski resorts double as downhill cycling courses in the summer. Courses include jumps and big drops.

◦ Mountain bikes designed for downhill racing have hydraulic disk brakes like the ones used in motorcycles and cars.

◦ Professional downhill bikes cost between £600 and £6,000.

◦ Bikes are made out of titanium.

Downhill cycling gear needs to be tough to protect the rider. In races, downhill cyclists reach speeds of more than 150 kph. **I hope they have good brakes!**

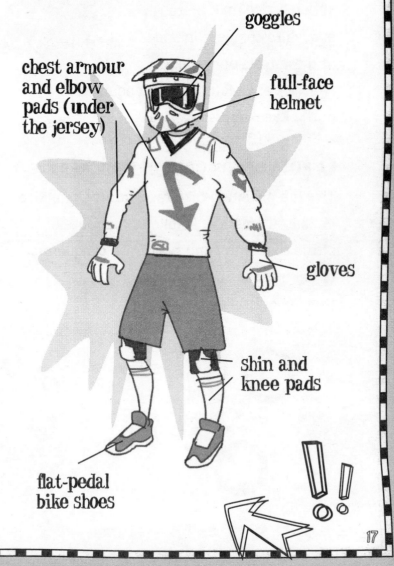

goggles

chest armour and elbow pads (under the jersey)

full-face helmet

gloves

shin and knee pads

flat-pedal bike shoes

Extreme Bike Races

Could you ever, **in your wildest dreams**, be tough enough to compete in one of these tests of cycling endurance: La Ruta de los Conquistadores or the Race Across America?

Wimp Rating: 8 out of 10

LA RUTA DE LOS CONQUISTADORES

This is a mountain-bike race across Costa Rica in Central America. It follows the route of two of the sixteenth-century Spanish conquerors of Central and South America (the Conquistadors).

Sound easy enough? It's 360 km long, from the west of the country to the east, and crosses the volcanic mountain chain that runs down the middle of Costa Rica — the peaks rise to more than 3,400 m.

Not put off yet? The race includes extremes of temperature — from tropical rainforests to freezing mountain passes — and competitors also have to deal with crossing rivers and active volcanoes.

La Ruta de los Conquistadores takes place every year in November over three days.

RACE ACROSS AMERICA

360 km? Pah! Race Across America is more than ten times that — 4,800 km — from the west coast to the east coast of the USA.

Most bike races, such as the Tour de France, have stages. Each rider is timed for completing one stage, then they have a nice rest before beginning stage two the following day. But the Race Across America laughs in the face of such **namby-pamby** ideas.

◎ The clock runs non-stop, so competitors try to keep going as long as possible. There are rules about the amount of rest riders have to take, but there are no afternoon naps!

⊘ Racers have a crew following them in a vehicle for safety reasons, and to provide food and water.

⊘ Riders can race on their own or as part of a relay team. Solo riders cover between 400 and 550 km per day.

Fastest Race Across America times:
Men — 8 days, 9 hours and 47 mins.
Women — 9 days, 4 hours and 2 mins.

FACTS WIMPS NEED TO KNOW

FASTEST BIKES

There are a whole range of racing
and mountain bike records:

◎ Flat surface (paced — towed by a
specially designed motor vehicle)

◎ Flat surface (unpaced — not towed)

◎ Downhill on a volcano

◎ Downhill on snow.

THE FASTEST SPEED EVER
RECORDED BY A BICYCLE ON
THE FLAT (UNPACED) IS ...
A) 95 KPH
B) 114 KPH
C) 133 KPH
D) 389 KPH

Answer: C). The other speeds are a) top speed of
an antelope, b) top speed of a cheetah, and d) the
top speed of a plummeting peregrine falcon.

◎ Markus Stöckl from Austria holds the world record for the fastest bicycle speed downhill on snow*, at 210.4 kph.

◎ The Dutch cyclist Fred Rompelberg holds the flat surface (paced) world-record speed at 268 kph.

*On a factory-built bicycle

23

BMX

BMX is short for bicycle motocross, because it's the pedal-power equivalent of motocross. There are five different types of BMX: street, vert, park, trail and flatland. Each one has it's own riding style and bike set-up.

Wimp Rating: 6 out of 10

BMX has been an Olympic sport since 2008. Riders compete on a track at least 350 m long.

The trickiest tricks include the 'No Footer', where after a jump the rider kicks their feet out to the side to make an 'X' shape, and combination tailwhips. For these the rider jumps and the whole frame of the bike rotates underneath while the handlebars point forwards!

BMX riders
are a worryingly
long way from the
ground when they perform
their tricks. The biggest ramp
used in competition — the X-Games
Big Air ramp — is 8.2 m high, and riders
whizz up it and into the air high above it.

TERRIFYING TRUE TALE

Professional BMX rider Mike Aitken crashed his bike in 2008 while he was riding with his friends. He was just doing a trick he'd done lots of times before.

Mike was in a coma for three weeks and suffered a brain injury, a broken jaw, a fractured eye socket and was paralysed down his right side. **OUCH!** He had to learn how to walk again, and lots of other things.

And the good news? Mike recovered! He's now riding, and even competing again.

Climbing

What on Earth possesses people to go clambering up mountains? Is it because:

   a) it's dangerous
   b) it's often extremely cold
   c) it's exciting
   d) it takes great skill

Answer: all of the above!

Most mountain climbers have all that safety equipment: ropes, harnesses, karabiners, etc. But there are some people who insist on going to extremes. You might want to skip the next section if you're afraid of heights...

(Don't look down!)

BELIEVE IT OR NOT...

In 2010, Jordan Romero became the youngest person ever to climb Mount Everest, the world's highest mountain, when he was just 13 years old. In December 2011, aged 15, he climbed Mount Vinson in Antarctica to become the youngest person ever to climb the Seven Summits – the highest mountains on each of the seven continents.

FACTS WIMPS NEED TO KNOW

FREE CLIMBING

Imagine yourself standing on a tiny ledge on a rock face, 600 m from solid ground, with the wind whistling in your ears, and no equipment to help you get up or down. . .

Wimp Rating: 9 out of 10

actually, don't.

It's far too scary!

Hey! That's my perch!

Free climbing is just like rock climbing, but without all the gear. Free climbers use only their hands and feet (they use ropes in case they fall, just not to help them climb). Free climbers aren't allowed to rest on ropes, or pre-place any climbing gear to help them. There's a list of rules to make climbing as difficult for them as possible.

FREE SOLO CLIMBING (SOLOING)

This is even more extreme: climbers don't use any equipment at all — there's no safety rope in case they fall, and if they make a mistake it's often fatal. They'd better not make any slip ups then!

BELIEVE IT OR NOT...

Alex Honnold is one of the world's best solo climbers. In 2008, he spent two hours 50 minutes becoming the first person to climb the northwest face of Half Dome in Yosemite, California, which is 600 m high. He climbed El Capitan, also in Yosemite, in just under six hours. It usually takes rock climbers at least two days to climb the same route.

Ice Climbing

If you're looking for more excitement than climbing boring old rock, you could try ice climbing. The good news is that you'll have harnesses and ropes and other mountain-climbing equipment. **Yey!**

The bad news is pretty obvious: you'll be climbing up ice — frozen waterfalls, glaciers and icy mountains — so it'll be completely and utterly freezing cold, and very slippery indeed. There's also the risk of falling into a crevasse or being buried under an avalanche.

TERRIFYING TRUE TALE

In 2012, David Warden was ice climbing on Britain's highest mountain, Ben Nevis. He and his climbing partner were scaling Zero Gully when they plummeted 400 m down the mountain. Miraculously, David survived — though he was badly injured. He shouted for help and was airlifted to hospital, where he made a full recovery. Sadly, his climbing partner didn't survive the fall.

Speed Skiing

Some people go to extreme lengths to get down mountains very fast indeed.

Wimp Rating: 9.5 out of 10

◊ Speed skiing is the fastest winter sport. Speed skier Simone Origone from Italy holds the world record at 251.4 kph (more than twice the speed limit on many motorways).

Is he ready?

◊ Speed skiing courses are 1 km long and horrifyingly steep.

◊ The snow is absolutely smooth — the slightest bump could send a skier spinning off course.

◊ Skiers plummet down the course at such speed that the air hits them with the force of a hurricane.

◊ Equipment for speed skiing stops skiers being flattened by the force of the wind: it includes super-streamlined helmets, airtight latex suits and triangular foam pads called fairings that attach to the backs of the legs.

◊ The fastest speed skiers accelerate as rapidly as a Formula One racing car.

◊ Skiing the course takes 15 seconds. Half of the course is for skiers to slow down and come to a stop.

MORE SPEEDY WINTER SPORTS

○ **The luge** — the record for the luge is almost 140 kph. Riders lie on a flat sledge, just centimetres above the ground.

○ **Speed skating** — these racers whizz along on ice skates at speeds of around 54 kph.

○ **Ice racing** — cars and motorbikes are fitted with studded tyres to race on frozen lakes.

A WIMP'S WORST NIGHTMARE

You gaze at the twisting, icy track in dismay.
When you agreed to be part of a bobsleigh
team of four, you hadn't realised the track
was so steep, or so long. And it's slippery too.
You've just been told that underneath that
layer of ice is solid concrete, that bobsleighs
can reach speeds of more than 200 kph, and
that a bobsleigh team was seriously injured
on this track last week. "Ready?" calls
your teammate. He shows you
where to push. There's no
going back now...

Suddenly you're pushing the
bobsleigh with the others. You leap
inside it when the pilot gives the signal.

Every bone in your body shakes as you go rattling down the track, faster and faster, at a death-defying speed that forces your body flat. As the bobsleigh turns almost onto its side, you're convinced it's out of control! **Aaarrrggh!**

BELIEVE IT OR NOT...
Georg Hackl, a luge gold-medallist, is also a champion wok racer: competitors race down bobsleigh runs on modified Chinese frying pans. (Chopsticks not required!)

Extreme Running

Lots of people like going for a run, but 42 km? It's a bit much, by most people's standards, and yet marathons and half-marathons are becoming more popular. Marathons got their name because of the Battle of Marathon, fought in ancient Greece in 490 BCE.

I think I have a blister...

Before the battle, a messenger from Athens, called Pheidippides, ran to Sparta for help against the Persians. He ran 250 km in two days, then ran another 40 km from Marathon to Athens to announce the victory. Once he'd delivered the victory message, Pheidippides dropped dead, which perhaps isn't surprising.

Answer: A). Believe it or not, Jennifer Amyx was five years old when she ran her first marathon in 1975 in Johnstown, Philadelphia, and she did it in under five hours. Bucky Cox was also five, but a bit older than Jennifer, when he became the youngest male marathon runner in 1978. Things were different in the 1970s, and it's probably just as well — young children wouldn't be allowed to run in an official marathon now.

EXTREME MARATHONS

Boggle your mind as you contemplate the runners for whom running a marathon is just a gentle warm-up. . . Every year a 250-km race called the **Spartathlon** recreates ancient Greek Pheidippides' run, except hopefully without the dropping dead bit.

Wimp Rating: 8.5 out of 10

START

The North Pole Marathon is run on Arctic ice floes, and is the only marathon not run on land. Runners endure freezing temperatures, with a wind chill of -25 degrees C. If you've run the North Pole Marathon, you could attempt to become a member of the North Pole Marathon Grand Slam Club, by finishing a marathon on each one of the seven continents of the world.

The Marathon des Sables (the Marathon of the Sands) is an ultramarathon run across the Sahara Desert in Morocco over six days.

It's considered the hardest foot race on Earth. Runners have to carry their own food for the whole six days in a backpack, though the organisers generously provide water and tents for competitors to rest in at the end of each stage. The whole course is 254 km long, and the longest stage is 84 km. The extreme distance isn't helped by the baking heat, which can reach up to 50 degrees C.

BELIEVE IT OR NOT...

In 1983, a 875-km race between Sydney and Melbourne in Australia, was won by a 61-year-old sheep farmer called Cliff Young, even though he was running against top athletes from all over the world. The other athletes stopped each evening to sleep, before continuing the race the following day, but Cliff kept going, day and night. He gave away the prize money to five other runners.

TERRIFYING TRUE TALE

Italian policeman Mauro Prosperi was running in the 1994 Marathon des Sables when a sandstorm blew up. As the swirling sand blurred the landscape, he became completely disoriented. He wandered lost and alone for nine days.

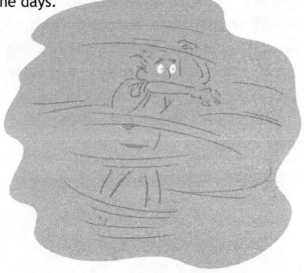

As he didn't have any water he survived by drinking his own wee, and eating snakes, scorpions, lizards and bats (which he discovered when he took shelter in a deserted Muslim shrine).

Eventually, in a state of almost total collapse, he met a nomad family. He found out he had wandered more than 200 km from the course, and was now in a completely different country: Algeria. He recovered, and has since finished the Marathon des Sables many times.

Triathlon

Not content with just running a ridiculously long way, some people have to show off by swimming and cycling as well, all in the same event.

The triathlon is an Olympic sport consisting of a 1,500-m swim, a 40-km cycle and a 10-km run, but different competitions use different distances — and of course the Olympic distances aren't nearly enough for some people. Lots of triathlons are held each year, but some are extreme even by triathlon standards. . .

Ironman* Triathlon

The Ironman Triathlon takes place in Hawaii every year. . . The swim is just under 4 km (it's in the sea,

but no wetsuits are allowed — they are for wimps). The bike ride is 180 km long (and it's hilly, with strong gusting winds). The run is the usual marathon length of 42 km (and it's raced in very hot conditions). Frankly, we're disappointed — call yourselves ironmen? A mere 4-km swim, and an ordinary marathon? Pah! Hang on, though . . .

CLUNK

CLANK

*Not just for men, women can take part too!

Ultraman*

There's an even more gruelling triathlon event, also held in Hawaii, with a proper run.

It's divided into three stages over three days. The first stage is a nice refreshing 10-km swim in the sea (yes, that's TEN km), plus a 145-km bike ride with steep climbs. The second stage is a 276-km bike ride including more steep climbs (just in case you thought 145 km was a bit tame). The third stage is an 84-km marathon (twice the usual marathon distance). **That's a bit more like it!**

*Ultraman is open to women, too.

BELIEVE IT OR NOT. . .

You don't have to wait until you're an adult to compete in rock-hard triathlon events. Ironkids is for children aged 6 to 15. It's not quite as brutal as the grown-up Ironman competition: the senior group (aged 12 to 15) compete in a 274-m swim, a 12.8-km bike ride and a 3.2-km run.

I'm training for the Ironkids competition.

I'm training to be a wimp!

EXTREME WATER SPORTS

Are you ready for some of the most exhilarating and dangerous water-based activities in the world? No? Neither are we. Stay on dry land and read the next chapter instead.

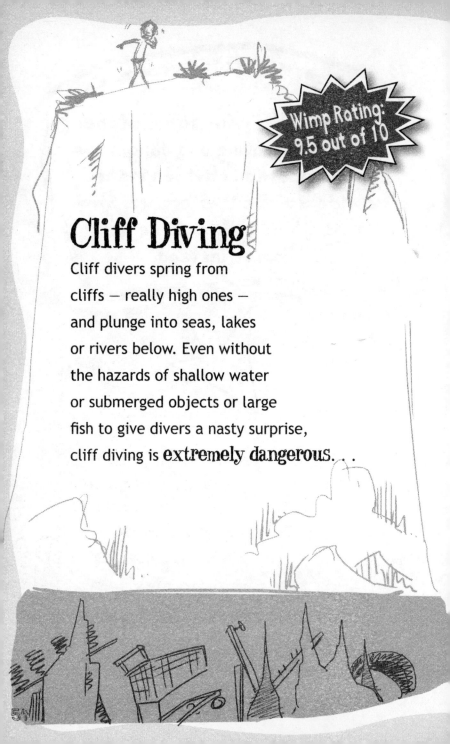

Cliff Diving

Cliff divers spring from cliffs — really high ones — and plunge into seas, lakes or rivers below. Even without the hazards of shallow water or submerged objects or large fish to give divers a nasty surprise, cliff diving is **extremely dangerous**. . .

BELIEVE IT OR NOT...

Cliff diving first became a competition because of an 18th-century Hawaiian king. In 1770, Kahekili was famous for jumping off high cliffs and into the sea below making hardly a splash. Kahekili insisted that his warriors did the same, to prove they weren't wimps.

His successor, King Kamehameha I, went a step further and made cliff diving (rather than jumping) into a competition – at least according to legend. The world's most famous cliff diving site, Kaunolu, is in Hawaii.

DANGEROUS CLIFF DIVING

In cliff-diving competitions, dives are from a
maximum height of about 26 m — that's like
standing on top of an eight-storey building.
From that height, divers hit the water at up
to 100 kph! Even if it's only water — hitting
anything at 100 kph is very dangerous. Divers
have to make sure they enter the water
absolutely straight, with pointed toes or hands.

The impact of diving from a great height is enough to compress the spine, break bones or give you a very nasty head injury. If the position of entry into the water isn't perfect, divers can be badly injured, or even die. The safest way to dive from great heights is feet first, but professional divers dive head first, and even perform somersaults or other tricks before making a streamlined entry into the water.

Cold water increases the stress on the body, and sea water is harder to dive into than fresh water because it's denser. The record for the world's highest dive is 52.42 m, held by Dana Kunze. A higher dive — 53.94 m — was made by Oliver Favre, but because he was injured and had to be helped out of the water, his record doesn't stand.

Extreme Swimming

Extreme swimmers won't make do with a few lengths of the pool — even an Olympic-sized one. They insist on swimming vast distances that take days to complete, encountering watery perils such as jellyfish, sharks, strong currents, extreme cold and huge waves.

> Slow down Martin, we can't keep up!

THE WORLD RECORD FOR THE WORLD'S LONGEST SWIM IS HELD BY MARTIN STREL, WHO SWAM...

A) 45 KM AROUND THE ISLAND OF MANHATTAN, NEW YORK

B) 233 KM BETWEEN ATHENS AND THE ISLAND OF SANTORINI IN GREECE

C) 808 KM BETWEEN HONG KONG AND THE NORTH COAST OF TAIWAN

D) 5,268 KM ALONG THE AMAZON RIVER IN PERU AND BRAZIL

Answer: D) of course! Martin has also swum the Yangtze River (4,003 km), the Mississippi River (3,797 km), and the Danube (3,004 km).

MARATHON SWIMS

The English Channel: The first person to swim the Channel, a distance of 34 km, was Matthew Webb in 1875. Since then around 1,200 people have swum the Channel — the youngest was 11-year-old Thomas Gregory, and the oldest was 70-year-old George Burnstad.

Erm...

Competitors keep out the cold by smearing themselves in goose fat or Vaseline or, in Matthew Webb's case, porpoise oil.

The Cook Strait: This marathon swim between New Zealand's North and South Islands isn't as far as the Channel — it's 22 km — but the waters are known for strong and unpredictable currents.

The Catalina Channel: this swim, between California and Santa Catalina Island, is 32.5 km wide and known for its sharks — but you're still far more at risk from exhaustion, dehydration, the cold and jellyfish. **So not to worry.**

Extreme Boats

Getting out of the
water and into a boat
seems like a very good
idea. Then again. . .

Wimp Rating:
8.5 out of 10

WHITEWATER KAYAKING

If you fancy paddling a boat along a
churning mass of white water punctuated
with jagged rocks, with only a few
millimetres of fibreglass to protect
you, whitewater kayaking is for you.

ROARRRRRRRR

There are six grades of difficulty: the first is just moving water with a few ripples in it, which sounds as though it could be attempted by even the most fearful wimp. But grade six is not for the faint-hearted: it means severe rapids and comes with the worrying warning **"danger to life or limb"**.

ATLANTIC ROWING

If you've ever rowed on your local pond and found it quite hard going, you probably don't want to compete in the Atlantic Rowing Race. Competitors row 4,700 km across the Atlantic Ocean, from the Canary Islands to the West Indies, in a journey that lasts more than six weeks (the fastest ever crossing took 36 days).

Some are in teams of two or four, while others attempt the crossing alone. They face enormous waves, driving rain and wind, plus the risks of exhaustion, dehydration or drowning if the boat sinks or competitors fall overboard.

Surfing

FACTS WIMPS NEED TO KNOW

THE PERILS OF SURFING

Think twice before you grab a body board
and paddle out to the breakers. . . The most
obvious hazards are the waves. Don't attempt
really big ones unless you're experienced.
A big wave can send you plummeting down
15 m as it breaks, not leaving you much
time to get to the surface and take a breath
before the next wave hits you.

◎ The pressure change can burst eardrums.

◎ Waves can fling you into reefs, rocks or the sea bed, causing serious injury or even death.

◎ Surf boards often give surfers a nasty bash, and the fin at the back of the board can cut flesh.

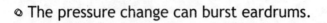

◎ Surfers use a leash to attach themselves to their boards, but the leash can become entangled in reefs or seaweed, and hold the surfer underwater.

◎ Surfers can be caught out by rip currents. Don't swim against a rip current, which could exhaust you — swim parallel with the beach until you're free of the current, then swim back to shore.

◎ Sea creatures! Sharks, stingrays, jellyfish. . .
for more information on scary sealife, see *The Wimp's Guide to Killer Animals*.

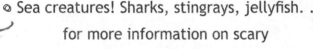

EXTREME SPORTS IN MID-AIR

If you're a true wimp, you're probably afraid of heights. So it might be best to read this next section with one hand covering your eyes, whilst holding on to a heavy piece of furniture with the other.

Skydiving

Wimp Rating: 8 out of 10

This extreme sport involves leaping out of a plane, helicopter or even the basket of a balloon, with a parachute — **for fun**. The really "fun" bit, at least according to keen skydivers, is the bit before the parachute goes up, when skydivers are falling towards the ground, thousands of metres up in the air. **(Seriously, what's wrong with these people?)** Once the parachute is opened, skydivers slow down and can control direction and speed using steering lines.

Hello! Looks like someone's dropping in for lunch...

WARNING
TIGERS

Some skydivers are determined to make falling out of a plane even more interesting...

Formations — groups of four, eight, sixteen or even bigger teams — grab hold of one another as they fall, sometimes forming patterns or standing on one another's shoulders, etc. The most people in a formation skydive involved 400 skydivers in Thailand in 2006.

Naked skydiving — **Erm...** Enough said.

squawk!

Skysurfing — skydiving with a surfboard or snowboard. It's like you're riding the air! Kind of.

Skydiving with a bike — the bike has to be ditched before the skydiver lands, so add 'being flattened by a skydiving bicycle' to your list of things to worry about.

Plane-to-plane skydiving — yes, that means jumping out of a plane, freefalling, and — somehow — climbing into a different plane! The list of reasons never to attempt this is a very long one.

WHICH OF THESE DIDN'T
REALLY HAPPEN?
A) SKYDIVING IN AN
INFLATABLE BOAT WHILE
SOLVING A RUBIK'S CUBE
B) SKYDIVING WITHOUT
A PARACHUTE
C) SKYDIVING IN A CAR
D) SKYDIVING WITH
JETSKIS AND KAYAKS

Answer: actually they all really happened. Travis Pastrana jumped out of a plane without a parachute, but two of his friends parachuted with him and he landed safely in tandem with one of them. Your list of "Things that Could Fall out of the Sky and Flatten You" just got longer.

Wingsuit Flying

Wingsuits are special
suits with webbing on
the arms and legs to
make the wearer feel
just like a bird. Well,

Wimp Rating:
8.5 out of 10

a bird that has to take off from a very high
cliff or jump out of a plane, in order to gain
enough height. And a bird that has to wear
a parachute — you can't slow down to a safe
landing speed with only a wingsuit.

Look, Mum!
It's Superman.
Look, Mum,
look! It really
is. Mum!

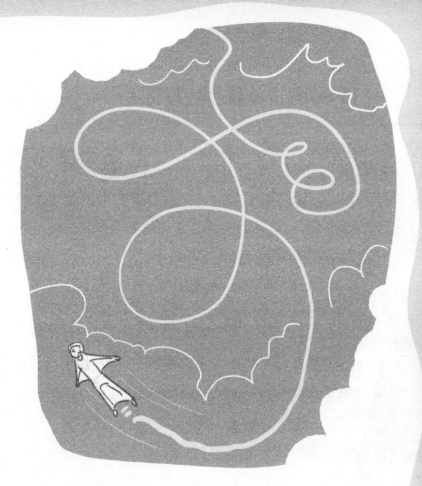

You can fly almost horizontally with a
wingsuit, and even perform aerial acrobatics.
The suit slows you down so that you fall much
more slowly than if you were skydiving. The
average skydiver plummets at around 190 kph,
while the average wingsuit flyer plummets at
around 90 kph.

BASE Jumping

Have you ever wanted to launch yourself off a very tall building or bridge, shouting "Geronimo!" as

you nose-dive towards the ground? Thought not. But apparently plenty of people do, hence the sport of BASE jumping. In case you're wondering why BASE always has capital letters, it's because it stands for Building, Antenna (tall towers), Span (bridges) and Earth (cliffs) — the four things BASE jumpers chuck themselves off.

Geronimo!

DANGER!

Obviously, BASE jumping is dangerous — **duh!**
It's even **more dangerous** than skydiving,
because BASE jumpers:

◌ have less control over their position and
can go into a spin,
◌ have less time to open their parachute,
◌ can be blown back against the object
they leapt from by high, swirling winds,
◌ have a small landing area.

Hi, officer

Been hanging around here long?

BELIEVE IT OR NOT. . .

In one of the riskiest BASE jumps ever, Anders Lau Nielsen and Chad Henderson both rode mountain bikes off a 1,000-metre cliff in Norway in 2012. They were fine, but the bikes went to pieces. . .

Bungee Jumping
A WIMP'S WORST NIGHTMARE

You knew you shouldn't have taken that dare. You look over the side of the Macau Tower and feel the blood drain from your face. Below you, the Zhu Jiang river glitters in the sun, a dizzying 233 m down. Someone is strapping you into your harness. You look at the clips and safety equipment. What if something goes wrong? You start to feel sick. "Come on," says someone, cheerily, "it's time to jump!" You gulp and look down — the ground far, far below seems to spin. You feel a pressure on your back and suddenly you're plummeting through the air. **"Aaaarrgggh!"** you scream, as your stomach lurches violently. . .

Why do they keep throwing themselves out of their nest?

WEEEEEEEEE!!!

BELIEVE IT OR NOT. . .

The people of Pentecost Island in Vanuatu, in the South Pacific, still perform the earliest form of bungee jumping in an annual ritual. They climb a 30-metre-high wooden tower and leap off it with vines attached to their ankles. A New Zealander called AJ Hackett watched the ritual and came up with the idea of bungee jumping as a result.

FACTS WIMPS NEED TO KNOW

BUNGEE JUMPING

◦ Bungee jumping means leaping off a fixed structure while attached to it by a length of elasticated rope. It began in the 1980s and, for some reason, became very popular.

◦ The highest bungee jump is at the Macau Tower in China. It's 233 m high, and jumpers plummet at up to 200 kph. There's a 4–5 second free fall, followed by a series of nauseating bounces as the elasticated rope springs you up and down before it comes to a rest. There have been serious injuries and deaths as a result of bungee jumping.

◊ Some of the biggest accidents have occurred because of equipment failure. Erin Langworthy, an Australian woman fell 111 m into crocodile-infested waters when her bungee cord snapped.

◊ There have been several cases where the cord used was too long for the drop.

◊ People have suffered problems with their eyesight because of the sudden change of pressure as you drop and bounce back again very quickly, and whiplash injuries due to the extreme jolt.

◊ You're less likely to be injured if you relax. So chill out — it's not as if you're about to jump off a tall building or something . . . **oh.**

IN THE FILM GOLDENEYE, WHAT STUNT DOES JAMES BOND PERFORM AT THE VERZASCA DAM IN SWITZERLAND?
A) HE ABSEILS DOWN IT
B) HE BASE JUMPS FROM IT
C) HE BUNGEE JUMPS FROM IT
D) HE DIVES FROM IT INTO THE WATER

Answer: C). The dam is 220 m high and, if you want, you can bungee jump from it between April and October every year.

Is the stuntman ready?

How far down is it?

Slacklining and Highlining

You've probably heard of tightrope walking, where people who should really know better balance on a cable above the ground, using a pole for balance. Slacklining is similar, but instead of a tight cable there's a slack nylon line that bounces like a trampoline as you walk along it.

Wimp Rating: 10 out of 10

You're probably thinking it sounds extremely
sensible. Maybe you can't wait to have a go.
Actually, it is fairly safe as long as you're not
very far from the ground. Most slackliners
string their lines between two trees close
to the ground, or above water, so that the
landing's nice and soft if they fall off (if a
little wet). But of course, there are people
who have to take their slacklines up higher...

HIGHLINING – THE STOMACH-CHURNING FACTS

Walking on a slackline high up is called highlining — and the lines can be very, very high. Highliners walk across their lines hundreds of metres up — for example, the Lost Arrow Spire in Yosemite National Park in California — its summit is 2,112 m.

Extreme highliners insist on wobbling about on slacklines hundreds of metres above ground without using any kind of safety line or harness. It's known as free solo highlining and it's not recommended.

BELIEVE IT OR NOT . . .

One of the world's best slackliners, American Faith Dickey, holds world records for women's highline, highline free solo, and longline – where the slackline is so long that every small movement makes the line bounce about like a horizontal bungee. One of her most death-defying stunts was walking a line tied between two trucks . . . which were hurtling – at speed and in a strong wind – towards two parallel tunnels. Faith had to walk across the thin line, battling to stay upright against the wind, before the trucks entered the tunnels and the line snapped on the dividing wall. She only just made it!

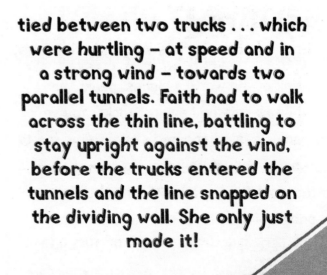

Last Word

You've been very brave. You've teetered on the brink of the world's highest peaks, and risked being smashed against rocks. You've brushed up against the perils of extreme sports — probably enough to keep you tucked up in cotton wool for ever. **Now you can relax.** No one's going to force you to climb up a frozen waterfall or run 250 km in the searing heat of the Sahara Desert. Actually, there are plenty of far more scary things for a wimp to worry about. . .

Come and give your nana a nice big kissy. . .

Your Wimp Rating

Answer these questions with "yes" or "no". How many do you answer "yes" to? Add up the number to generate your very own wimp rating on page 93 – go on, how tough are you really?

Wimp Rating: ?? out of 10

1. You're at the beach when someone says you should go out on a board to catch some waves – hey, it's only water after all. You say. . .

2. Martin Strel invites you for a quick swim. You say. . .

3. A friend has just been given a wingsuit for her birthday, and offers to let you test it. You say. . .

4. You win a competition to join Faith Dickey on her latest record attempt. You say. . .

5. You think La Ruta de los Conquistadores is a gentle bicycle ride. You say. . .

7. A friend has pulled out of the Atlantic Rowing Race with an injury. Do you take his place?

8. You'd be happy to enter an Ultraman event.

9. The X-Games Big Air ramp is for babies on tricycles.

10. You'd be happy to jump off a bridge with only a piece of elastic tied to your legs.

How many questions did you answer "yes" to?

Three questions:
you're a novice wimp – you're on a sloping trail to wimp excellence.

Four questions:
you're a wannabe wimp – banish those extreme sports thoughts!

Five questions:
you're a splash away from wannabe status.

Six questions:
you're marathon mad for extreme sports.

Seven questions:
you speed ski through life.

Zero questions: you're the Ultimate Wimp – superb! You have truly embraced your inner wimp.

One question: you're a mega wimp – a perfect example of extreme wimpness. Well done!

Two questions: you're a champion wimp – give yourself a gentle pat on the back!

WIMP-O-METER

Eight questions: you swoop through sports challenges with a wingsuit.

Nine questions: you're as high-wired as a highliner in the Himalayas.

Ten questions: too tough! You're not even a weany bit wimp-like – but you are slightly nuts! You'll have to dig deep to find your inner wimp.

Glossary

abyss an extremely deep hole or gap between rocks

adrenalin a hormone (chemical) produced by the body when you are frightened, angry or excited

compress squeeze

crevasse a deep crack in an ice sheet or glacier

current in the sea, a body of water moving in a particular direction

dehydration extreme thirst

designated official named (footpath, in this case)

gruelling requiring hard work

hydraulic disc brakes these use brake fluid to operate

karabiner a metal safety clip used on climbing ropes

mountain chain a connected group of mountains

mountain pass a route over a mountain

nomad someone who does not live in one place but moves from place to place to find fresh grazing for animals

rapids fast-flowing section of a river

titanium an extremely strong, light metal

vertical straight down

vine climbing plant

wetsuit close-fitting item of clothing made of rubber and worn by swimmers to keep them dry/warm

whiplash injury to the neck caused by a sudden jerk

Index

The Wimp's
Guide to

illustrated by
Dave Smith

Jungle
Survival

by
Tracey Turner

978 1 4451 1461 3 pb   978 1 4451 1465 1 eBook

Have you ever:

Paddled down the Amazon River? ✕
Been stung by a scorpion? ✕
Gone without food for a day? ✕

If you answered NO to all of the above then this is the book for you!

Terrified of bugs? Great! Feel sick about travelling? Fantastic! Inside you can read about loads of crazy stuff and how to survive – or avoid it.

Love your inner wimp!